I'm So Glad You Stayed

The True Story of Ringo Star-ling

Written and Illustrated by

Dixie Frank

Prologue

I have always wanted to write and illustrate a children's book. The sudden loss of my mother, and the rescue of the baby European Starling who I named Ringo, inspired the writing of this story.

Ringo had fallen about forty feet from his nest in the barn and somehow survived. Much research, hourly feedings and fretting resulted in Ringo thriving and becoming a much loved member of our family of two humans, two dogs and two cats.

Ringo occupies a sunny room where he is free to fly every day. He takes a swim at least five times a day and then preens himself to perfection.

He sings, whistles and talks all day long. One of his favorite songs to whistle is the theme to *"The Andy Griffith Show"* and of course he whistles *"Dixie"*.

You can see more of Dixie's art work at
www.designsbydixie.net

For Mom
Forever missing you and your smile.
Thank you for always encouraging me to fly.

Once upon a summer day, a tiny baby bird called a starling poked his way out of an egg, in a nest, high in an old barn. He lived there with his mom, dad, brothers and sisters.
As the newly hatched babies grew, the nest became very crowded. The young starlings all wanted to be the first to eat when mom and dad returned to the nest with their meal.

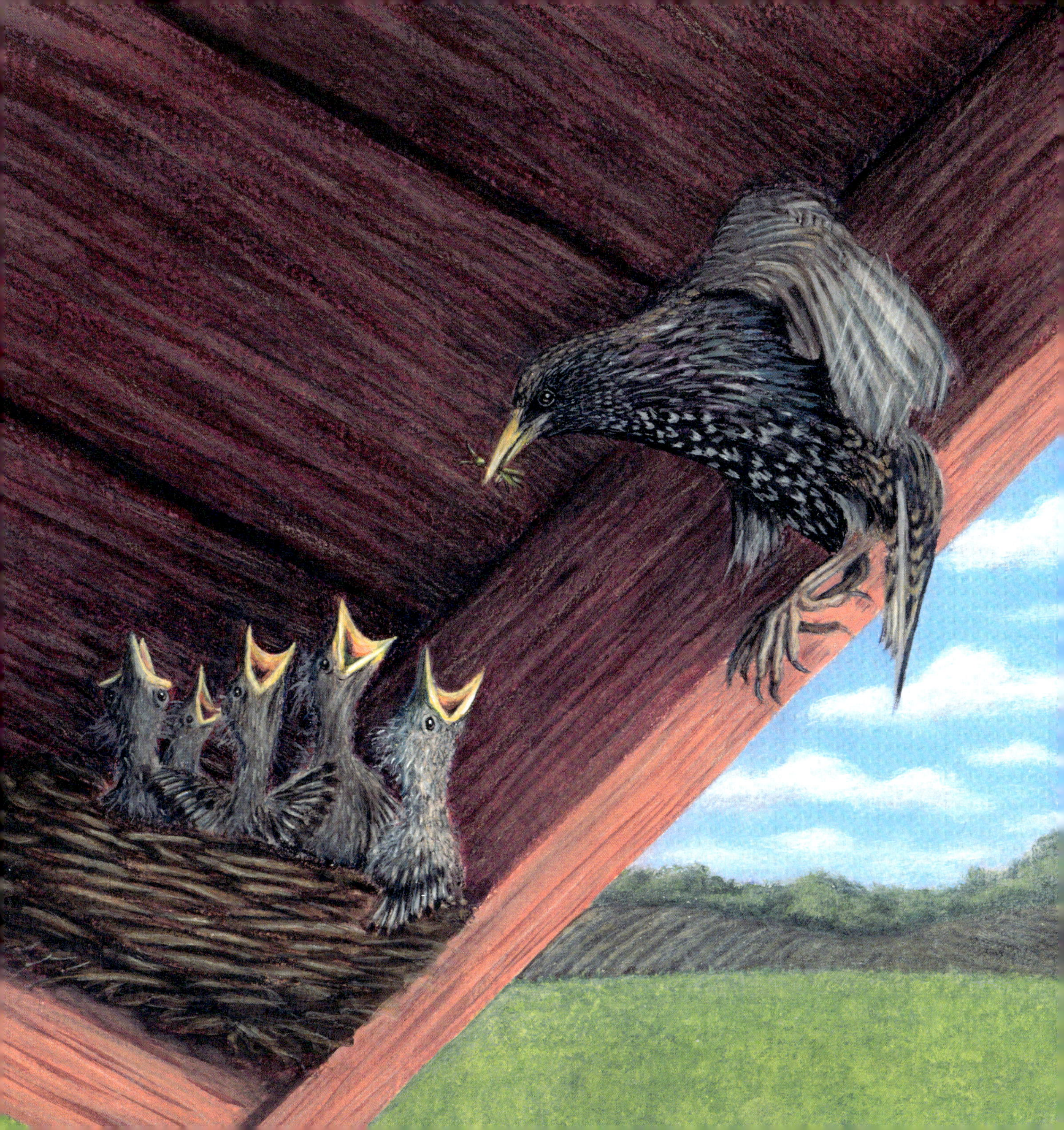

One morning as the tiny birds pushed and shoved to get their food, the smallest of the babies was pushed right out of that very high nest! Fortunately for the little starling, a breeze caught him and gently floated him to the green grass below.

The frightened little bird lay in the grass wondering what to do. He had only a few feathers and could not fly back to his family high up in the nest.

"I wish someone would save me!" he cried.

Just then, a very large hand reached down and scooped up the fuzzy little bird. He was a kind looking man who wore a bright red hat.

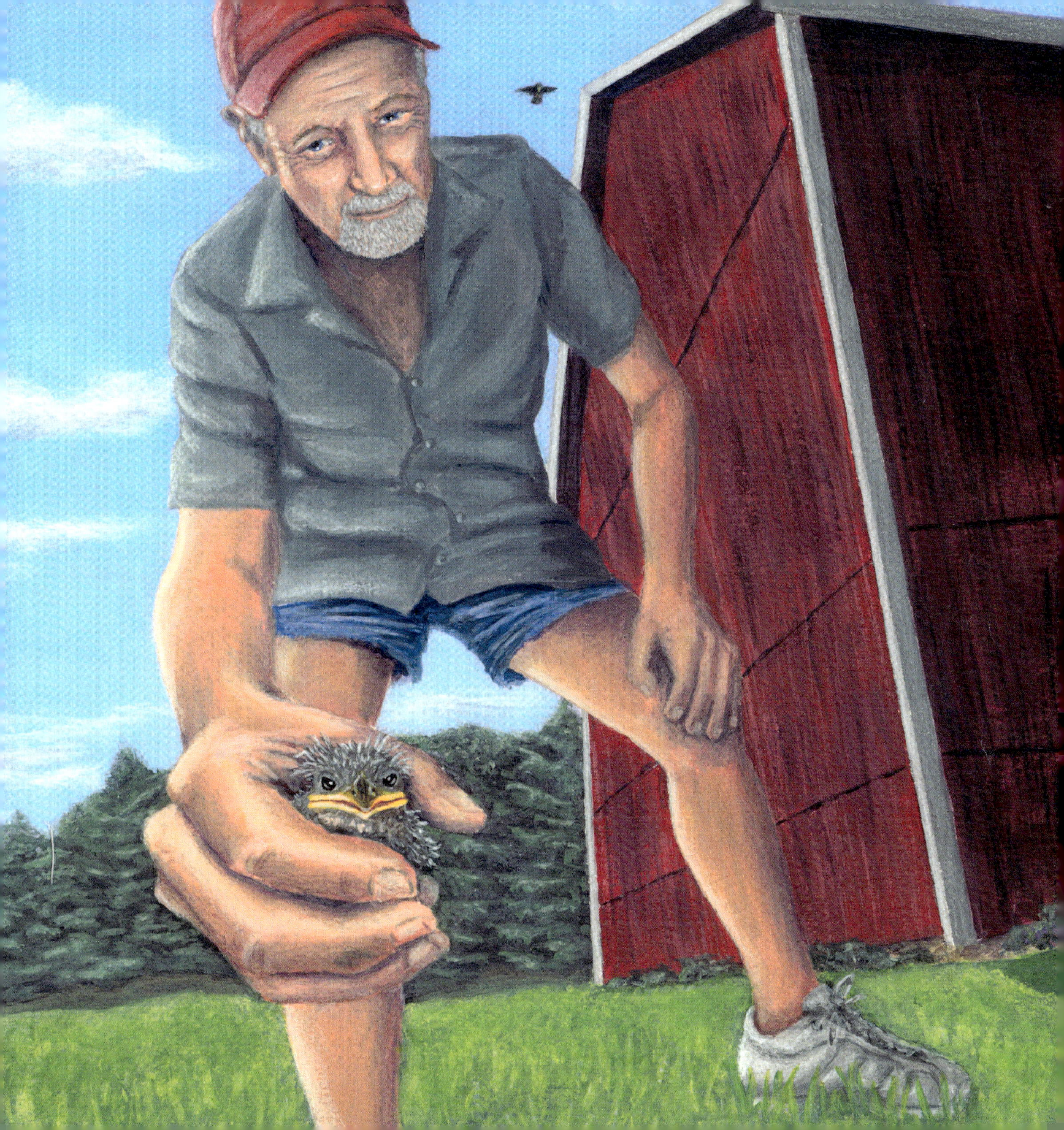

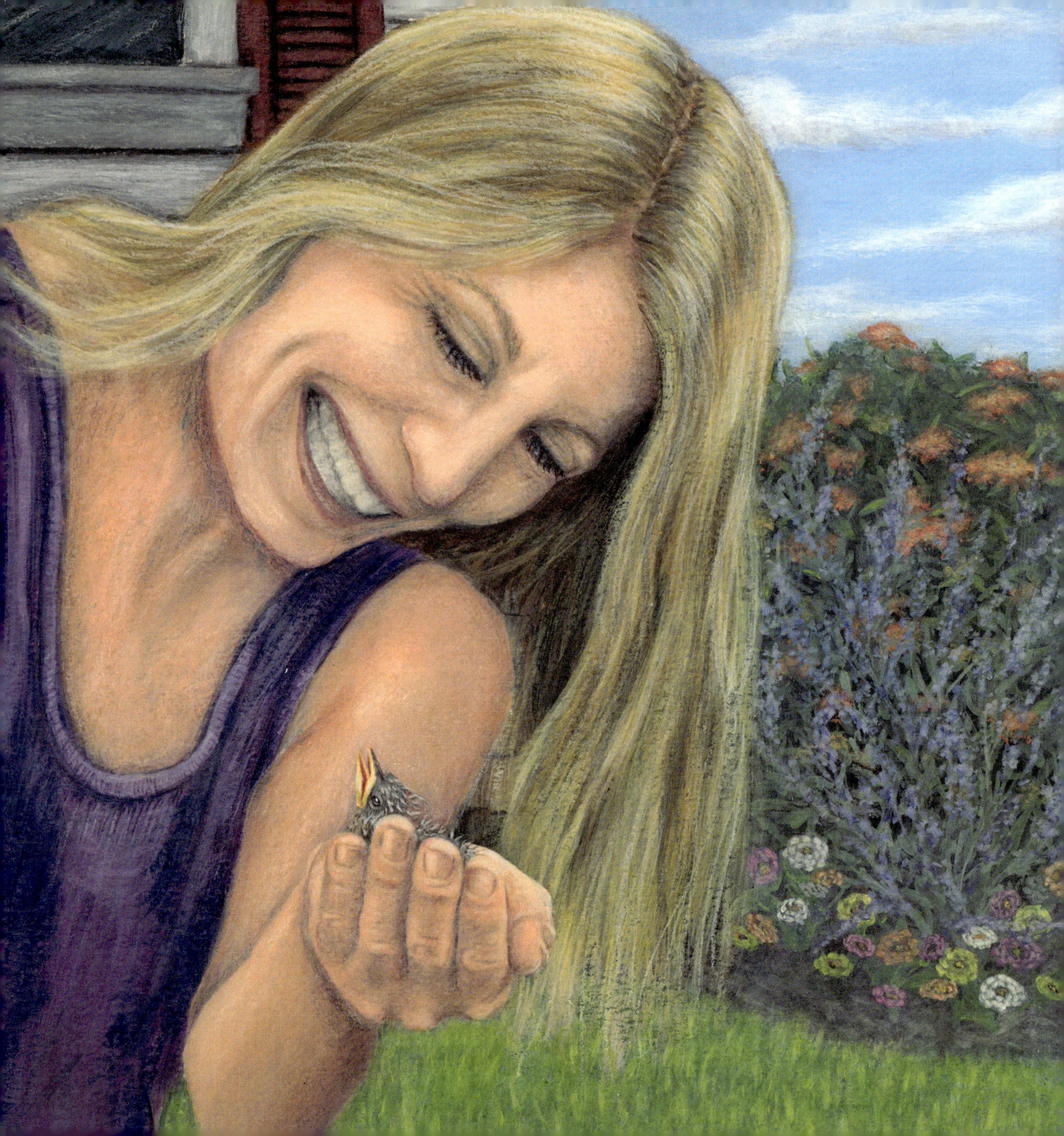

The man carried the baby bird up to the house and handed him to a lady with big blue eyes. Instantly, she loved the helpless baby starling with all her heart.

Together, the man with the bright red hat and the lady with the big blue eyes fed and cared for him. They named him "Ringo Star-ling".

Soon he was living in a big cage decorated with swings, toys and even a swimming pool! "I'm so glad you saved me!", he thought.

Ringo grew very quickly and within days learned to fly.

He would fly back and forth to his new mom and dad, landing on each of their heads again and again.

When he was tired of flying, Ringo would take a swim in his pool and splish splash water everywhere!

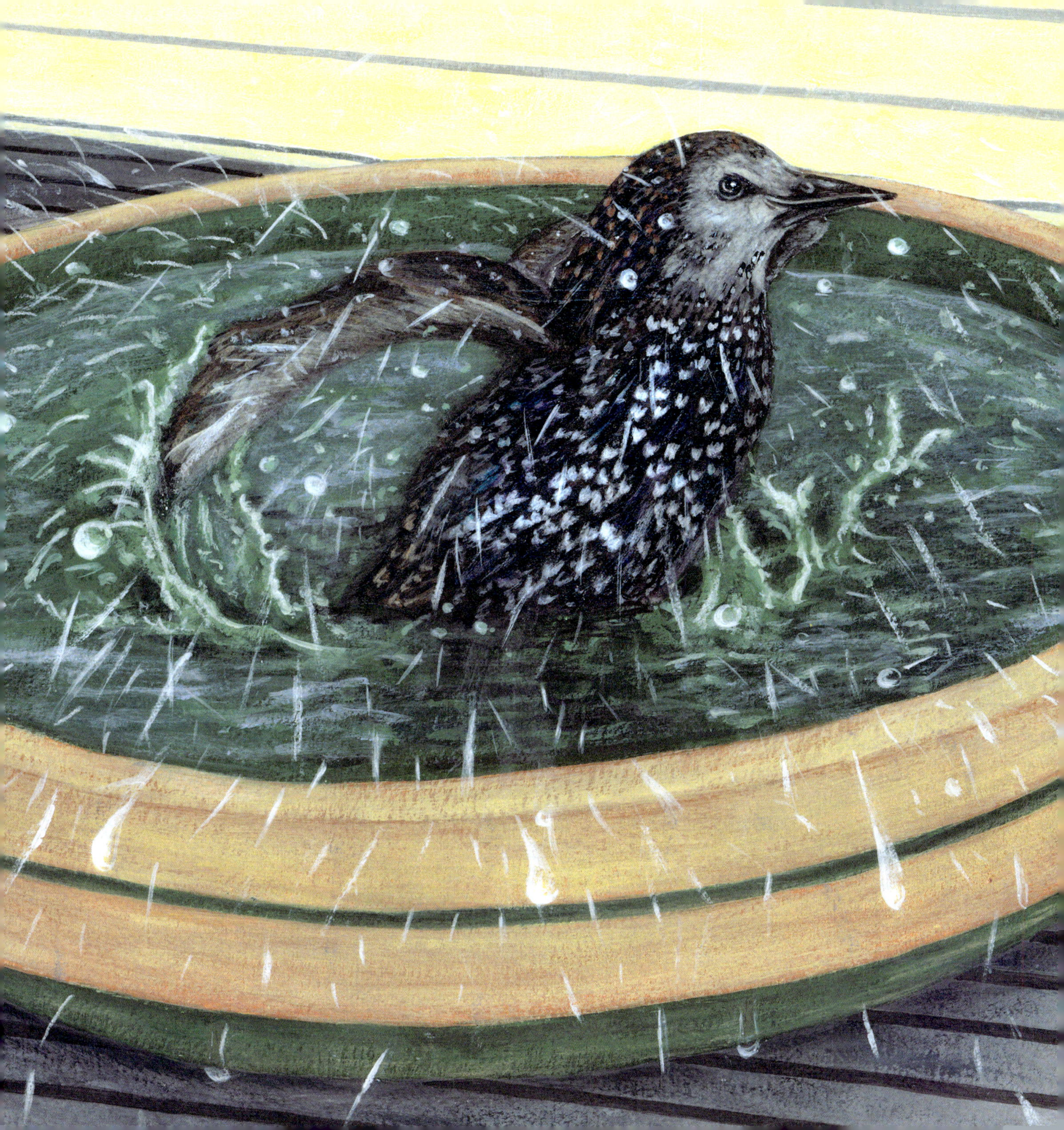

Ringo's new mom and dad loved to spend time playing with him. They talked to him, made funny noises and even sang to him.

Music always played in his new house and Ringo loved music. Before long, he was whistling along with some of his favorite songs.

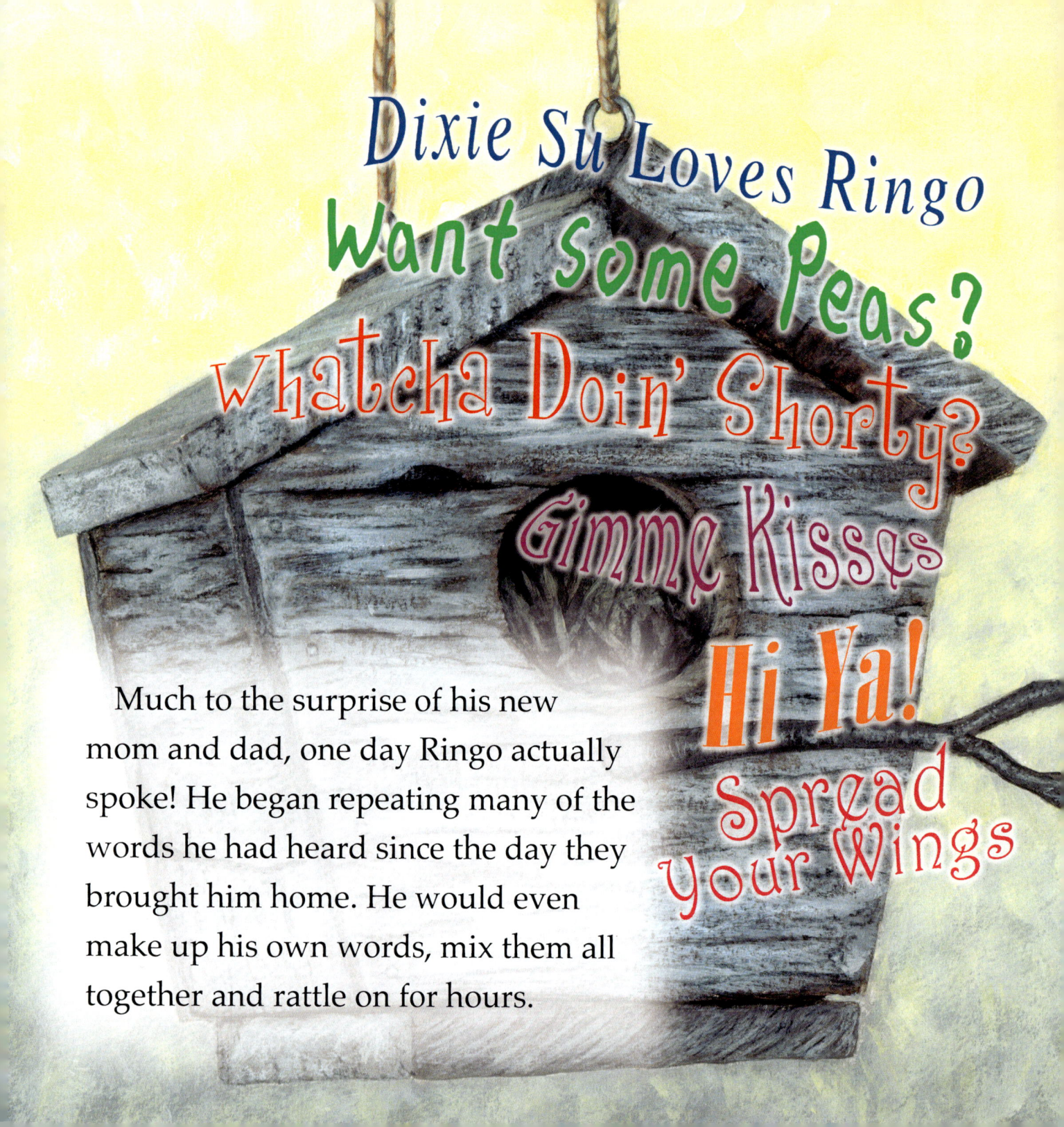

Dixie Su Loves Ringo
Want some Peas?
Whatcha Doin' Shorty?
Gimme Kisses
Hi Ya!
Spread Your Wings

Much to the surprise of his new mom and dad, one day Ringo actually spoke! He began repeating many of the words he had heard since the day they brought him home. He would even make up his own words, mix them all together and rattle on for hours.

FLY BOY!
Ring Ring Ringo
Go Swimmin'?
Go Splish Splash?
Good Morning!
Hop Up There, Go On!

On mornings when the sun streamed in the window, Ringo would perch on his new mom's arm, fluff up his feathers, spread his wings and take a little rest from flying. The warmth of the sun and the love he felt from his new mom made him happy.

"I'm so glad you saved me" he sighed.

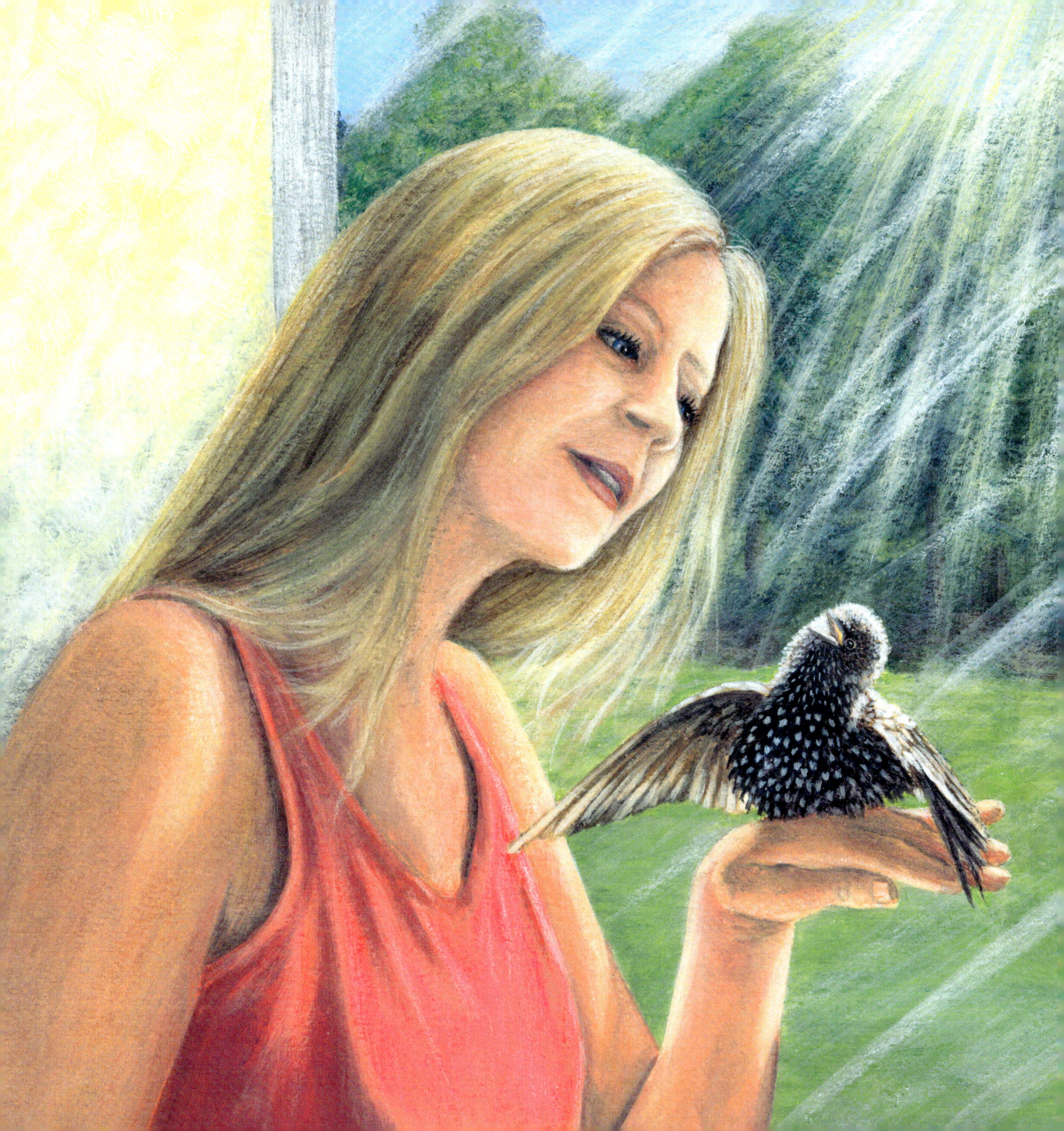

Ringo looked out his window and saw starlings and other birds flying past. Even though he was very happy with his new mom and dad, he still thought about his other family, high in the nest in the old barn. Where are they now, he wondered? He missed his mom. Would he ever see her again? It made him sad to think about the family he had lost.

Ringo's new mom understood what he was feeling. She had lost her mom too and missed her very much. Some days she wondered if anyone could save her from the sadness she was feeling.

While sunning on her arm one day, Ringo looked up and saw a tear run down her cheek.

"We were brought into each other's life for a reason, Ringo" his new mom said. "The day you fell from your nest, high in the old barn, you needed me to love and care for you. When I was feeling sad and alone, loving and caring for you was what I needed. You have made me laugh and smile every day. Thank you Ringo, for falling into my life.
I'm so glad you saved me."

Just the Beginning

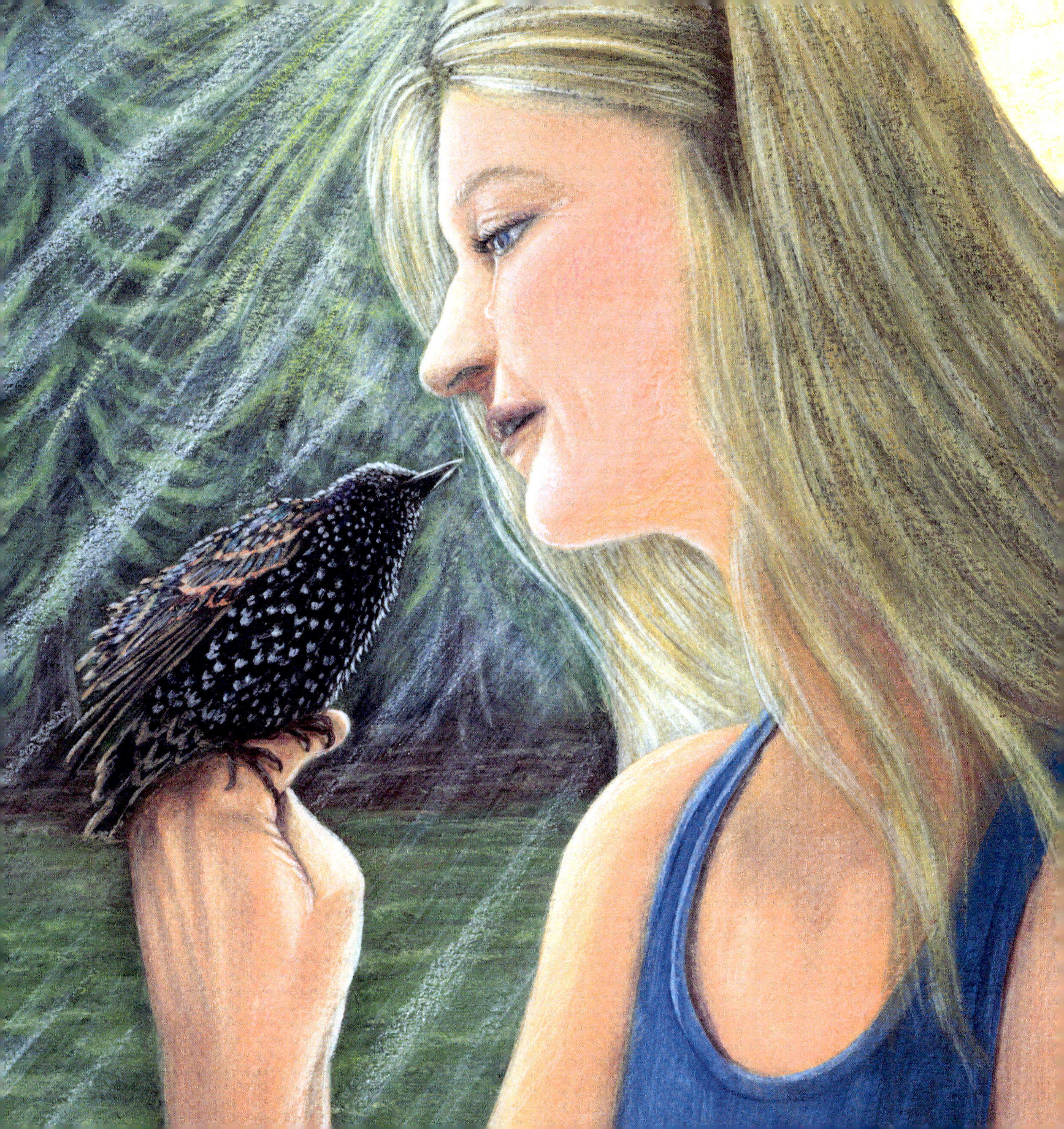

Starling Facts

European Starlings *(sturnus vulgaris)* were brought to America by Europeans in the 1890's. About 100 birds were released in Central Park in New York City. The group of people that released them wanted America to have all the birds that William Shakespeare wrote about.

Mozart had a pet starling that he wrote a poem about and composed music for.

Today there are more that 200 million starlings reaching from Alaska to Mexico. They are considered pests by many people.

Starlings can fly at speeds up to 48 mph.

In the wild, starlings can live to be 15 years old or more. Domesticated, they can live to be over 20 years old.

Wild starlings eat insects, berries, worms, various grains and seeds and just about anything they can find. Domesticated starlings have a very specific diet that you can learn about on www.starlingtalk.com

The white spots on the starling's chest are called stars.

The male and female are very difficult to tell apart. The base of the beak may be more bluish on the male and more pinkish on the female.

Male starlings are the nest builders. The male and female both incubate the eggs. The nests can be built within 3 days and can be as high as 60 feet off the ground.

Starlings can mimic the songs of other birds as well as the human voice. They are very social, amusing birds that bond very quickly with their humans.

A flock of starlings flying in unison (all together) is called a murmuration. Thousands of starlings group together creating patterns in the sky like acrobats.

If you find a baby starling needing care, one that may be injured, or simply want to know more about these intelligent and amusing birds, visit the website www.starlingtalk.com.

Thanks and Acknowledgments

Thank you to my kind looking man in the bright red hat. When you found him, you knew I would do everything possible to help the little guy.

A huge thank you to the Starling Talk website for existing and making Ringo's survival possible. Without you, we would have been as helpless as he was.

The Fact Page information is also courtesy of these websites.
www.starlingtalk.com.
www.allaboutbirds.org

To all my family and friends who listened to the story over and over and assured me it was worth telling and illustrating.

To Clem, my senior art instructor (1979), for being my friend and most trusted critic.

To Matt Scherler for his photography for the back cover art and website.
www.photographytraditions.com

To Ringo, for being the inspiration for my first children's book and teaching me so much about our feathered friends.

Copyright © 2014 by Dixie Frank

This is a work of nonfiction

All rights reserved by the author, including the right of reproduction in whole or in part in any form.

Blossom Book Publishing
A Division of Blossom Marketing & Publishing, LLC

Medina, OH

CF@blossomBookPublishing.com
Or by calling 330-723-6166

ISBN 978-0-9893583-3-0
Library of Congress Control Number 2014931061

CPSIA information can be obtained
at www.ICGtesting.com
Printed in the USA
BVXC01n1649010414
349353BV00002B/4